DRAGONS

DO YOU BELIEVE?

This series features creatures that excite our minds. They're magical. They're mythical. They're mysterious. They're also not real. They live in our stories. They're brought to life by our imaginations. Facts about these creatures are based on folklore, legends, and beliefs. We have a rich history of believing in the impossible. But these creatures only live in fantasies and dreams. Monsters do not live under our beds. They live in our heads!

45th Parallel Press

Published in the United States of America by Cherry Lake Publishing
Ann Arbor, Michigan
www.cherrylakepublishing.com

Reading Adviser: Marla Conn MS, Ed., Literacy specialist, Read-Ability, Inc.
Book Design: Felicia Macheske

Photo Credits:© Kiev.Victor/Shutterstock.com, cover; © Potapov Alexander/Shutterstock.com, 1;
© TUM2282/Shutterstock.com, 5; © Sylphe_7/iStock, 7; © KobchaiMa/Shutterstock.com, 8; © fortuna777/
Shutterstock.com, 11; © FairytaleDesign/iStock, 13; © Tomasz Kobiela/Shutterstock.com, 14; © Artorn
Dumkram/Shutterstock.com, 17; © Tereshchenko Dmitry/Shutterstock.com, 19; © Volodymyr Burdiak/
Shutterstock.com, 20; © quadshock/Shutterstock.com, 23; © bluedog studio/Shutterstock.com, 24;
© Renata Sedmakova/Shutterstock.com, 27; © Laslo Ludrovan/Shutterstock.com, 29

Graphic Elements Throughout: © denniro/Shutterstock.com; © Libellule/Shutterstock.com; © sociologas/
Shutterstock.com; © paprika/Shutterstock.com; © ilolab/Shutterstock.com; © Bruce Rolff/Shutterstock.com

45th Parallel Press is an imprint of Cherry Lake Publishing.

Library of Congress Cataloging-in-Publication Data

Names: Loh-Hagan, Virginia, author.
Title: Dragons : magic, myth, and mystery / by Virginia Loh-Hagan.
Description: Ann Arbor : Cherry Lake Publishing, [2016] | Series: Magic,
 myth, and mystery | Includes bibliographical references and index.
Identifiers: LCCN 2016004924| ISBN 9781634711135 (hardcover) | ISBN
 9781634713115 (pbk.) | ISBN 9781634712125 (pdf) | ISBN 9781634714105
 (ebook)
Subjects: LCSH: Dragons—Juvenile literature. | Animals, Mythical—Juvenile
 literature.
Classification: LCC GR830.D7 L5835 2016 | DDC 398.24/54—dc23
LC record available at http://lccn.loc.gov/2016004924

Cherry Lake Publishing would like to acknowledge the work of The Partnership for 21st Century Skills.
Please visit *www.p21.org* for more information.

Printed in the United States of America
Corporate Graphics Inc.

TABLE of CONTENTS

Chapter One

Ferocious Fire Beasts

What do dragons look like? What are the different types of dragons?

"Here be dragons." This was written on one of the world's oldest globes. Dragons were here before people. They're magical beasts. They make fire!

They have giant lizard or snake bodies. They have large bat wings. They have four legs. They have scaly skin. They have horns. They have fangs. They have long tails. They have claws. They have thick spines.

They live on land. They live in the sky. They're different from sea monsters. Sea monsters live underwater.

Dragons were first found on the eastern coast of Asia.

Explained by Science!

Dragons shouldn't be able to fly. It doesn't make sense. Their weight is too much for their wing size. They're like bees. In the 1930s, French scientists said it was a mystery that bees fly. Bees have small wings. Their wings can't produce enough lift to get them in the air. Scientists were baffled. Then they figured it out. They realized bees' wings aren't stable like a plane's wings. Bees flip and rotate their wings. They fly more like helicopters. They bend their wings. They rotate them quickly. They have a fast wingbeat. They take short, choppy wing strokes. They have light and hollow bones. They work hard to fly. They work like racing cars.

Dragons live all over the world.

Western dragons come from Europe and America. They're powerful. They're also evil. They fly. They destroy towns. They burn houses. They snatch humans. They snatch animals. They eat **prey** whole. Prey are victims.

Western dragons live deep inside caves. They sleep during the day. They hunt at night. They have big leathery wings.

They're greedy. They **hoard** treasure. Hoard means to store and not share. They steal gems. They steal gold.

Eastern dragons come from Asia. They're called **lung** dragons. They're smaller. They don't have wings. They have long whiskers. They have lion faces. They have **manes**. Manes are hair around their faces. They have snake bodies. They have deer antlers. They have eagle claws. They have tiger paws. They have fish scales.

They control water. They live in caves. Their eggs are giant pearls. They protect these pearls. They eat fish and swans. They change shape. They shrink. They stretch. They disappear.

They're good. They're lucky. They bring good fortune. They fight evil.

Chinese dragons control the rain, rivers, lakes, and sea.

Black dragons are evil. They live in swamps and jungles. They drown prey. They spit **acid**. Acid is a poison that burns.

Red dragons only care about treasure. They live in mountains. They live on islands. They eat **maidens**. Maidens are pure women.

Blue dragons live in deserts. They have one horn. They do surprise attacks. They blast lightning.

Green dragons live in forests. They torture prey. They spit out poisonous gas. Little horns cover their heads.

White dragons are small. They're smart. They live in cold places. They freeze prey. They blast ice.

There are different species of dragons. Species are groups.

Chapter Two

Beware of the Beasts!

What are the powers of dragons?
How do dragons attack?

Dragons have deadly weapons. They make **toxins**. Toxins are poisons. Toxins are in their mouths. They make fire. They make acid. They make ice. They breathe out these things. Their breath can kill.

Most dragons make fire. Their fire can be 1,000 degrees Fahrenheit (538 degrees Celsius). This is really hot. Dragons make fire in a second. They do it without thinking.

Dragon fire destroys whole cities. It burns people alive. It burns animals alive. Dragons cook their own food!

It looks like dragons are breathing fire, but they're making it in their mouths.

Dragon blood is powerful. It comes from dead dragons. Evil dragon blood has poison. It seeps through metal. One drop causes death. Good dragon blood has healing powers. It heals cuts. It heals sickness. It makes people stronger. It makes people healthy. It makes people smarter.

Dragons can control minds. They make people do things. They turn people into slaves. Their spell can last several months.

Dragons are smart. They speak many languages. They speak in riddles. They play word games.

Dragon blood can make human skin invincible. This means it can't be harmed.

When Fantasy Meets Reality!

Komodo dragons live in Indonesia. They look like dragons. They're the world's biggest lizards. They're 10 feet (3 m) long. They weigh 200 pounds (90.7 kilograms). They have scaly skin. They have long tails. They have long claws. They see well. They're fast. Their spit has many germs. It also has venom. Venom is poison. Komodo dragons have over 60 teeth. Their teeth have jagged edges. They're deadly. They bite and inject venom into their victims. They'll eat almost anything. They'll eat humans. They wait for prey. They attack throats. They wait for the venom to kill prey. They tear large chunks of flesh. They swallow it whole. They throw up horns, hair, and teeth.

Some dragons, like Hydra, have many heads.

Dragons have super senses. They hear well. They smell well. They see really well. They have cat eyes. They easily spot gems and prey. They can see 6,000 feet (1.8 kilometers) away. They have several eyelids. This protects their eyes while flying.

They're built for fighting. Their wings have small fingers. This means they can climb walls. They have hard scales. This is like armor. Nothing can hurt them. They have sharp claws. They rip. They tear. They gore. Their tails are strong and long. Tails are used to strangle prey.

Chapter Three

Dragon-Slaying

**What are the weaknesses of dragons?
How can dragons be slayed?**

Dragons have weaknesses. They're not **immortal**.
They don't live forever. But they live a long time.
They live for thousands of years. They age. They get
older. They lose power. They lose scales. Missing
scales exposes skin. These are areas that can be cut.

Their eyes are soft spots. Their bellies are soft.
But dragons sleep on treasure. Gems and gold stick
to their bellies. They act like armor.

There are many stories about heroes and knights slaying dragons.

Some stories say dragons fear elephants.

Their heads can be chopped off. This stops dragons from breathing fire.

Dragons are magical. So, magic can be used against them. Magic can stop them. It can't kill them. There's a taming spell. There's a cooling spell. These spells require things like unicorn hair. Spells can be dangerous.

Many dragons hate the sun and moon. They can cause an **eclipse**. An eclipse is when the moon moves in front of the sun.

SURVIVAL TIPS!

- Take cover. Or get a shield. Dragons drop things from tall buildings. Protect your head.

- Be prepared. Get your weapons. Get fit.

- Don't wear any jewelry. Dragons want jewels. They'll kill you to get them.

- Try to be friends with dragons. Offer them treasure.

- Don't take advice from a dragon. They like to trick people.

- Ask permission to ride a dragon.

- Don't look into a dragon's eyes. Dragons can control you.

- Don't interrupt dragons while they're counting jewels. This makes them mad.

- Wear fireproof clothes. Wear a fireproof face mask. Don't get burned by dragon fire.

Chapter Four

From Eggs to Beasts

How are dragons born?

Dragons start out as eggs. The eggs are 4 feet (1.2 meters) long. They're the same color as the mother dragon. Eggs have oval shapes. They have hard shells. They're like stones. They take years to hatch.

Dragons' nests don't need to be soft. Dragon eggs are strong. They're not easily broken. But they must be kept warm. Mother dragons blow a flame over the eggs. They do this every four hours.

The dragon **chicks** grow inside the eggs. They grow an egg horn. This is a sharp tool. It helps them crack the eggshells.

Any creature that eats a dragon egg will become a dragon.

Mother dragons lay eggs every 30 years. They lay a few eggs.

A **hatchling** eats the other eggs. This is why there aren't many dragons. Hatchlings are baby dragons. They're newly born.

Hatchlings have soft scales. Their scales are like feathers. They slowly harden. Hatchlings are weak. They're helpless.

Dragons are born with their mother's memories. They don't remember being born. They believe they've lived forever.

A dragon's life cycle is similar to a lizard's.

Know the Lingo!

- **Basilisk:** snakelike dragon with a deadly gaze

- **Crest:** a decorative ridge of spikes found on dragons' necks, backs, or tails

- **Dragonmetricity:** the practice of measuring dragons

- **Dragonology:** the study of dragons

- **Frost dragons:** dragons that move from the North to South Poles and breathe ice

- **Knuckers:** dragons that can't fly

- **Lair:** a dragon's home

- **Lindworm:** a long, wingless dragon that walks on two legs

- **Marsupial dragons:** Australian dragons that carry their babies in pouches

- **Scute:** bony plate or scale

- **Serpents:** snakelike monsters

- **Shew stone:** crystal ball

- **Smuggler's tales:** local legends about dragons to keep people away from treasure

- **Wyvern:** a dragon with wings, two legs, and a barbed tail

Chapter Five

Dragon Lore

What are some stories about dragons?

Fu Hsi was a Chinese hero. He was half human. He was half snake. He was the first to meet a dragon. This happened in 2962 BCE. The dragon taught Hsi many things. Hsi learned to write. He learned math. He learned music. He learned to fish. He learned how to tame animals. Then he taught other people.

Herodotus lived in ancient Greece. He wrote about dragons in 450 BCE. He saw flying creatures. He saw large dragon bones.

Dragons appear in nearly all cultures.

Real-World Connection

J. P. de Kam is like a human dragon. He's a professional fire-breather. He's also an experienced BASE jumper. He combined his two passions. He did the first fire-breathing BASE jump. He was on a 500-foot (152 m) cliff. A cliff is a steep or overhanging mountain edge. He was in Lauterbrunnen Valley. It's in Switzerland. Over 30 BASE jumpers died in this valley. But he wasn't scared. He wore a fuzzy animal suit. He drank "dragon fuel." Fuel is liquid that starts fires. He grabbed a torch. He jumped off the cliff. He lit his mouth on fire. He blew out flames. He dropped down. The fire trail followed him. He did a spin. Then, he pulled his canopy. A canopy is a special parachute. It's like an umbrella. It slowed him down as he landed.

In the Middle Ages, dragons were depicted as evil. Saint George was a famous dragon slayer. A male dragon bothered a town. The dragon made the town give him a maiden each year. The dragon ate the maiden. George found out about this. He stopped the dragon. He made the sign of the cross. He used his **lance**. A lance is a sharp pole. He put a leash around the dragon. He took the dragon to town. He used his sword. He slayed the dragon. He saved future maidens.

Good or evil, dragons are exciting!

People were knighted for slaying dragons.

Did You Know?

- Dragon dung can be rubbed into skin. It fixes skin problems. It can be used in gardens. It helps plants grow really fast.

- Dragon teeth can be used for weapons. They're sharp. They're strong. They're unbreakable.

- Dragon scales can be melted down. They turn into invisible ink.

- Marco Polo was an Italian explorer. He said he saw dragons.

- Many people think dragons are related to dinosaurs.

- China has fossils. Some people think these are "dragon bones." They take the bones. They grind them into powders. Some Chinese doctors use these bones. They make medicines.

- Ancient Celtic people worshipped dragons. They thought dragons were wise and powerful. They believed dragons could see the future. They thought dragons guarded the gates of hell.

- Dragon comes from the ancient Greek word *draconta*. It means "to watch." This suggests that dragons are guards.

- The Chinese zodiac has 12 animals. Dragons are one of the animals. It's the only mythical animal. Every 12 years is the year of the dragon. It's a lucky year. People born in this year are great leaders. They also have long lives.

- People thought rain clouds, thunder, and lightning were dragons' breath.

- Cadmus was a mythical king. He used dragon teeth to build an army. He threw dragon teeth in a garden. He waited for soldiers to grow.

Consider This!

Take a Position: Some believe dragons are the most powerful monsters. Read other books in 45th Parallel Press's "Magic, Myth, and Mystery" series. Which monster do you think is the most powerful? Argue your point with reasons and evidence.

Say What? Read the 45th Parallel Press book about Hydra. Compare what you learned from that book to what you learned from this book. Explain how Hydra is similar to dragons. Explain how Hydra is different from dragons.

Think About It! People used to think the world was flat. Dragons were said to be at the edge of the world. Pictures of dragons were common on early maps. They marked unexplored areas. They served as warnings. Why would people be afraid of these areas? Why would people be afraid of dragons?

Learn More

- Drake, Ernest. *Dragonology: The Complete Book of Dragons*. Cambridge, MA: Candlewick Press, 2003.

- Legg, Gerald, and Carolyn Scrace (illustrator). *Dragons*. Mankato, MN: Book House, 2014.

- McCall, Gerrie. *Dragons: Fearsome Monsters from Myth and Fiction*. New York: Tangerine Press, 2007.

- Sautter, A. J. *A Field Guide to Dragons, Trolls, and Other Dangerous Monsters*. Mankato, MN: Capstone Press, 2015.

- Welch, Laura, Bodie Hodge, and Bill Looney (illustrator). *Dragons: Legends and Lore of Dinosaurs*. Green Forest, AR: Master Books, 2011.

Glossary

acid (AS-id) poison that can burn through things

chicks (CHIKS) baby dragons inside eggs

Eastern (EEST-urn) the eastern part of the world, like Asian countries

eclipse (ih-KLIPS) when the moon moves in front of the sun

hatchling (HACH-ling) newly born baby dragon

hoard (HORD) to collect and store without sharing

immortal (ih-MOR-tuhl) ability to live forever

lance (LANS) long, sharp pole used as a weapon

lung (LUHNG) Asian dragon

maidens (MAY-duhnz) pure women

manes (MAYNZ) hair around the head and neck

prey (PRAY) victims, those hunted for food

toxins (TAHK-sinz) poisons

Western (WES-turn) the western part of the world, like Europe and North and South America

Index

About the Author

Dr. Virginia Loh-Hagan is an author, university professor, former classroom teacher, and curriculum designer. She loves dragons! She was born in the year of the dragon! She lives in San Diego with her very tall husband and very naughty dog-dragons. To learn more about her, visit www.virginialoh.com.